HOW INTERESTING CONVERSATION WORKS

*BREAK THE ICE, TALK TO STRANGERS &
WIN YOUR FEARS + BREAK THE ICE,
APPROACH AND FLIRT WITH WOMEN
Win Your Fears, Be Confident And Attractive.
Start Flirting And Pick Up Girls With
Magnetic Charisma (2 Manuscripts)*

Steve Lowndes & Ian Leil

The content contained within this book may not be reproduced, duplicated or transmitted without direct written permission from the author or the publisher.

Under no circumstances will any blame or legal responsibility be held against the publisher, or author, for any damages, reparation, or monetary loss due to the information contained within this book. Either directly or indirectly.

Legal Notice:

This book is copyright protected. This book is only for personal use. You cannot amend, distribute, sell, use, quote or paraphrase any part, or the content within this book, without the consent of the author or publisher.

Disclaimer Notice:

Please note the information contained within this document is for educational and entertainment purposes only. All effort has been executed to present accurate, up to date, and reliable, complete information. No warranties of any kind are declared or implied. Readers acknowledge that the author is not engaging in the rendering of legal, financial, medical or professional advice. The content within this book has been derived from various sources. Please consult a licensed professional before attempting any techniques outlined in this book.

By reading this document, the reader agrees that under no circumstances is the author responsible for any losses, direct or indirect, which are incurred as a result of the use of the information contained within this document, including, but not limited to, —

errors, omissions, or inaccuracies.

TABLE OF CONTENTS

HOW INTERESTING CONVERSATION WORKS

BREAK THE ICE
TALK TO
STRANGERS
& WIN YOUR FEARS

Steve Lowndes & Ian Leil

CHAPTER 1:
HOW DO YOU START A CONVERSATION WITH SOMEONE?

For a variety of reasons, which can be getting to know more new people, trying to build a relationship with someone or just having a good time that night and an enjoyable experience, very often people ask themselves:

"How do I start talking to someone in a bar?"

"How can I talk to that girl at the party?"

"How do I make friends with that person at that event?"

Now, truth be told, yes, there may be specific differences in the way that you will want to talk to these people depending on the scenario.

But, the thing is that most of the time what really happens is that you end up just standing there thinking about all the different possible things you could say without actually taking any action.

When the time comes, when it's time for you to say something, you are blocked by a myriad of thoughts and you don't say anything.

Let's say that you had a general method of approach that you could use on anyone, anywhere, to start a conversation.

It would be great right?

Well then just allow me to show you how it's done.

I will teach you three methods to strike a conversation with anyone that will become so natural to you that they will turn into just a reflex so that you will be able to finally speak up and meet some interesting people.

Without getting lost in chitchat, let's dive straight into it: this is how you can easily and successfully start a conversation with anyone.

CHAPTER 2:
THE MENTAL SEARCH METHOD

The first method we're going to see is used to make a practical change in the way you start a conversation with someone, by affecting your mindset.

We call it "The Mental Search Method": let's see how it has anything to do with conversations and how it will change your mentality.

Why "The Mental Search Method"? You know the way you would search for words or facts on Google? Great, you have to do the same thing but in your head.

Let me explain this a little bit more in depth.

Nowadays whenever you want to know something, you won't ask someone else directly or say it out loud, you will most likely look it up online.

If you want to know the best restaurants in the area, you will check them out on yelp or tripadvisor and so on.

But what if you did actually ask someone else? Isn't that a super easy yet effective way to engage in some small talk?

I remember for example the other day when I was at the gym, there was going to be a big football game that night and as someone new in the area, I had no idea where to watch it. So I just randomly asked a guy and just like that we spoke for a good 10 minutes and I ended up meeting up with him that night at the pub to watch the fight.

So the trick is, ask all those questions that come up in your mind out loud to people around you or directly to the person you want to talk to.

You can practically use this technique with anyone; we advise that you use it with people you don't know at all, to practice your technique and to make sure that you use it more and more naturally.

Obviously to start it is also fine with groups or people you know.

Let's make another example.

I recently moved to Beverly Hills. Nice place. I really like it.

This is what I did to start getting to know people there:

The first question you want to ask to a person or people nearby is: "Do you live here?"

You could say, for example, "What's the reason why you like it so much here?" or "If you had to convince someone who just moved here to stay, what would you tell them to visit?"

In this way, you will be able to not only meet new people or entire groups of people, you will also discover new places, create new relationships, make new friends or even just have a chat with a stranger for a few minutes.

I'll give you another scenario. Imagine that you're walking somewhere and suddenly you hear someone speaking a language you recognize or you even speak yourself (it really doesn't matter if you don't, showing interest and curiosity is more than enough).

You could just ask them, for example, "Hi, where are you from?" "Are you a tourists?" "Are you visiting here?".

You might think that these are stupid and trivial examples, but there is an important lesson in all this, which we will explain more in depths later on:

It doesn't matter how you start a conversation, the truly important thing is how you continue it. Therefore, the first thing you say is of little to no importance (unless you offend the other person, which we wouldn't honestly suggest).

CHAPTER 3:
THE TRUE SECRET TO KEEP THE CONVERSATION GOING

The goal after starting a conversation is to keep it up.

The way you can continue your conversation is what creates a real bond with that new person or group of people.

Here's another little secret for you, what truly matters is to lead the conversation towards the emotional plane, and then ask the other person variations of the question "How do you feel" (right now or about something and/or someone).

So, let's go back to one of the previous examples.

We broke the ice but we will truly only engage in a real conversation from the moment we ask that very important question "how do you feel?".

So we could ask someone "How do you feel about tonight?" "Are you excited about what's happening?" "What do you think about this and that?"

This way you will deepen your bond with your interlocutor and will start creating a connection based on feelings towards something.

"How do you like it here? What's your favorite thing?" when you ask them a feeling question that's when we get to people's sensations and feelings, that's when the real one-on-one game begins and we can keep the conversation interesting, engaging and fluid.

This connects directly to our second method: this is what we will call the twitter method.

If we use google to ask questions, twitter is where we go to make a statement.

I was at a club the other night.

At one point I see a person dressed in a very shiny suit who looked almost like an astronaut.

Basically, I grabbed the person who was standing right next to me and I said, "Hey, you gotta see this one. An astronaut just walked right into the club!"

And that's it, that's really how simple it is, after that we started talking and our conversation started.

Now, the fundamental point of these methods you're discovering is that you should not be going to the person or group of people you're interested in and try to start a conversation with a question or phrase you've already planned before or you have been thinking about for hours.

The problem a lot of people have is that they sit there thinking and thinking, looking for something to say without actually taking any action.

Overthinking never helps in these spontaneous situations.

Many people think they should break the ice with a compliment, and then they just get stuck thinking about what they should even compliment or how to phrase it.

And let's be honest, say that you want to open your conversation by complimenting someone's outfit and they're just wearing a white t shirt and jeans. Chances are your comment will not sound credible or genuine at all.

But when you put aside that fixation for searching at all cost for the right thing to say, which often turns out to be useless effort, and you simply go with the flow of genuine thoughts going through your head, you will always have something to say that no matter how stupid, silly or trivial it may seem at first, will allow you to start talking to someone.

I can't stress this enough, the real focus of the conversation, what really matters, is not what you say at first.

Believe it or not, there are countless people out there who can't wait to have a conversation with someone…

So next time you're out there thinking, "Oh my God, it's so hot today, I'm roasting", just say it out loud. Boom, twitter method.

It's very likely that someone close to you will say something like, "Yes this is unbelievable, it's so hot, isn't it? "

Now you can level the field right away.

You can continue with "It's absurd, isn't it? I don't know if I can take it. I was almost thinking about moving somewhere else, what do you think?"

And that's really it, remember that an emotional response is what you are truly looking for.

When you get to talk about each other's feelings, you're starting to have a real conversation…

27

CHAPTER 4:
THE THIRD TECHNIQUE

The third method is something very effective in closed social settings and the best part is that it's nothing more than a simple sentence.

Virtually we are talking about any kind of environment really, a club, a bar, your university and so on.

The unconscious expectation of any kind of person or group of people who attend these places is to be social, and therefore to talk to people.

As a result, these are systematically great places to be social with other people.

The method is quite simple: you go over to a person (even in a group) and you tell them: "Hey, I don't think I've met you yet. I'm Fred", while reaching out for a handshake.

It's really that simple.

It's a technique that works almost always and it's great because it communicates unconsciously a number of things about yourself to the other person.

First of all, it shows that you are a sociable person, since you're practically starting the conversation in a very natural way.

Secondly, it makes it clear that people should know each other in these contexts and that it's weird that that person has not gotten to know you yet.

It's like saying, "You know, I don't think I've met you yet, we should have definitely met by now."

As a reflex, people will shake your hand as you reach out to shake theirs, they will follow you and be interested in what you say.

Again, what you'll want to do next is connect to the feelings of the person you're talking to, by asking questions such as, "are you having fun? What do you like about this place? What brings you here tonight? "

This way, you'll start the real conversation and your relationship will deepen creating a superficial bond.

Remember, don't worry too much about how the conversation starts. Just start it and dive straight into it.

We still want to give you more ways to continue your conversations so that you don't have embarrassing moments of silence and you can always have something to say even when you're in trouble, so now we'll cover how to make small talk.

CHAPTER 5:
SMALL TALK

We'll now give you simple and effective methods to use to engage in small talk with anyone, to make your conversations fluid, easy going and fun so that the person you are talking to will like you almost instantly!

What's the point of making small talk?

The function of small talk is to keep a conversation going successfully and to prevent it from getting stuck in a dead end.

The goal of making small talk is still the same as doing conversation: to check if you can get along with a person, to see if you can have a relationship of sort with that person, or to see if you like that person or not. As a result, you can create friendships, deeper bonds and romantic relationships.

Without getting lost in chitchat, we will immediately see some simple and effective ways to make small talk and to be liked straight away by the people we talk to.

CHAPTER 6:
SURPRISE THEM

The first method, that usually surprises most people, is to go for a compliment plus a cold-read of the person you are talking to.

The other day I was chatting with a group of people I had just met. I made a joke and a girl just naturally said "Oh you're so funny, are you a comedian?"

She very positively surprised me, I really appreciated her comment and it made me like her right away, after that we started talking and I explained to her more about my job as a writer and motivational speaker.

That was a great example of both a cold read, so a blind guess on someone based off their actions or something they said, followed by a compliment.

You can make guesses about what they do, where they come from, what hobbies they have... and so on...

And believe me, it's far better than just asking questions as if it was an interview. Such as "So what is your job?" or "What do you do in your free time?"

There's no comparison.

It can really be anything, like, "Wow, you've such good taste in clothing, I bet you're a stylist.", "You are so convincing, you must be a great seller.".

If you guess correctly, they'll be even happier, they'll laugh and wonder how you knew. That means more bonus points for you.

But if you don't, it's okay, you will positively surprise the person you're talking to and make them like you right away.

It's a great method to get rid of the interview vibe, giving the conversation a fun pace. You make a guess, compliment them and as a consequence they will start telling you what they actually do or where they come from etc etc.

In addition, it is very likely that they will be much more involved in the conversation and they will show much more engagement and appreciation towards you.

CHAPTER 7:
THE AVALANCHE TECHNIQUE

The second method to progress after engaging in small talk is to create an avalanche of words, and in the midst of it, throw in a good question. Creating an avalanche is definitely an appropriate move after giving a Cold-Read.

The goal here is to ask a good question, it doesn't matter how simple, to put the other person in a position where they'll want to talk a lot.

This will make the other person feel really involved in the conversation, and it will ensure that you avoid getting those one-word answers you get when the other person is not really interested in the conversation.

So, the other person will be so excited about the question you asked them that they'll answer with a cascade of words.

There are two ways to achieve this reaction, that will work even better if combined together:

First of all you have avoid any question you can answer to with a yes or a no or that has no possible follow up whatsoever.

For example "For how long have you lived here?"

That's a question that's both trivial and that can end a conversation right then and there.

Most of the time people can just reply "10 months", "1 year" or other other answers along those lines.

Remember that you have to emotionally engage them by getting their feelings involved in order to create interest in the conversation.

"What do you like to do for fun? or "Why did you move here?" are both much more open questions that leave room for much longer answers, as well as make the other person talk about their own feelings.

The second key point is to ask them a question they are unconsciously waiting for and therefore they will want to answer, because it's about a topic they like.

It is very common among people to ask, for example, "Hey how's work?" This is a classic question that will generate a one word answer "good / bad / fine" and that will be the end of the exchange.
But if you get their feelings involved too, their answers will change drastically: "Hey, what's cool at work these days?" (this will push them towards talking about

something they like or dislike about their job, a project or a co worker or who knows what else) or "hey, how are you spending your free time lately, what do you do for fun?" or even "Is anything exciting happening in your life right now?"

In addition to creating a positive atmosphere, there will be a better connection between the two of you and the person you are talking to will feel much more involved in the conversation.

CHAPTER 8:
THE GUESSING GAME

The third method for the most effective small talk is to play a guessing game.

The premise is to avoid doing this all the time, so not after every sentence, but first let's see what it actually consists of:

If you realize that you are about to ask one of those trivial routine questions such as "Where are you from?", you can turn it into a guessing game right away by saying something like. "Wait, wait, give me a couple of hints and let me see if I can guess."

They will now have to give you two hints and by thinking about those tips they will already be more involved in the conversation, plus they will appreciate the fact that you are trying to make the conversation more fun.

So, while you're guessing, you will also find yourselves joking and laughing.

Finding out where they are from will be a lot more fun this way.

It is a very useful method in most social situations and in various contexts such as bars, clubs, or any closed place really. Go for it whenever you think it is appropriate (use your common sense) it's a fun and refreshing way to ask instead of using the classic routine questions that feel so much like an interrogation of the FBI.

It's also much better than having the conversation go on and on about traffic, the weather, or other monotone subjects.

Let's face it, people always end up talking about that and it's boring.

CHAPTER 9:
GIVE ME YOUR ADVICE

The fourth and last method for successful small talk is to ask the person in front of you for an opinion on a topic you're interested in.

You will not necessarily have to keep talking about this topic but they will appreciate you asking for an opinion or advice and listening to them.

This will show them that you give importance and value to what they tell you or what they think.

This is all about asking a simple question about what you honestly think is interesting, and it's really nothing more than saying "Hey, I have a quick question for you, what do you think about...this or that?"

Unlike the second method in which we ask a question that you think could be interesting for them, here we ask a question about a topic of interest for us, based on what we like.

You can also play a little bit with them, for example, by asking a girl at the bar a question like: "Hey, which shirt do you like better, mine or his?" (pointing at some other random person at the bar) and after their answer playfully say: "Ah come on you're just saying that because you like him more than me, it's not the shirt."

This is guaranteed to create a fun and relaxed atmosphere.

If you want to keep the conversation more serious and discover something about the other person's way of thinking, say for example that they are married or divorced, you can ask something along the lines of "Hey, I've been together with my fiance for a while now and I've never been married, in your opinion, what makes a long-term relationship work?"

They will be excited to answer whether they have a successful marriage behind them or not, because people always have a tendency of giving tips to avoid mistakes they made themselves.

In this way you will be able to get an idea of the person's way of thinking, as well as make that person open up to you and it's much better than the usual trivial questions like "how's work going" or "what are you doing" etc.

CONCLUSION

Breaking the ice and approaching someone new is demonized and looked at as an insurmountable problem to solve.

In reality it is nothing like that and it should come as natural as possible.

Fixing your habits and improving your technique using the methods I illustrated in this book will do wonders.

Get back in action and never feel awkward again.

Try out these tricks and improve your social skills!

Best of luck see you in the next book.

BREAK THE ICE, APPROACH AND FLIRT WITH WOMEN

Steve Lowndes & Ian Leil

INTRODUCTION

I'd like to start my book off by congratulating you for deciding to take action and improve your skill and level of success with women by reading this book.

Too many men think that in order to be attractive or to flirt properly what is going to make a real difference is exclusively their bank account and being handsome.

This is far from the truth. Surely attractive or rich people have certain features that women find attractive but you need to read between the lines and not just stop at their appearance.

Taking care of yourself and the way you present yourself is incredibly important but it's NOT just looks that make a difference.

A lot of men come up to me and say "Steve, I'm not handsome, there's no way I will ever get a girl. I'm just not hot enough".

I want you to think about it and try understand the reason why attractive and rich men REALLY get women.

What they truly have is confidence and awareness around women.

They BELIEVE that any woman will like them and this is reflected in their behaviour, they may even be too cocky at times which isn't great as you always want to find the right balance to achieve the best success rate.

If you're serious about learning how to flirt, you will soon realize that any man with regular features and an ordinary bank account will be able to enjoy the company of a woman he thought would always be way out of his league.

Flirting is a skill. I will not sugarcoat it for you, it's going to be tough at the start, as any new skill always is when you are learning it for the first time, but with some practice and a few fails you will find your own rhythm and style.

With that being said, this is Steve Lowndes and welcome to my flirting short course.

CHAPTER 1:
THE EYE CONTACT RULE

The first ever study about how men and women perceive creepiness has been completed recently with some very interesting results.

Men and women experience creepiness differently. Men think of creepiness as scary movies, the supernatural, clowns, and all spooky things of sort.

Women associate it to those same things plus one more.

Can you guess it?

Men. They think of men as creepy.

It's not hard to believe, throughout the course of every man's life, as we are flirting, I'm sure each one of us has done something creepy that made a woman really uncomfortable at some point.

I know I definitely have in the past and that's mainly because we don't perceive creepiness the same way women do so most of the time we might not even realize we are doing something creepy.

With this book I want to save you the trouble of trying to understand what's creepy for a woman and directly explain to you the most common ways guys are creepy without even realizing it.

I live in L.A. and the first incorrect thing I notice guys doing all the time, especially in the club, is how they make eye contact.

In general creepiness follows the Goldilocks rule: too little or too much of something are both bad.

You will need to get it just right.

This applies to eye contact, I'm sure you all know what too much eye contact looks like, when you are literally staring at someone. Or when a man gets right up in the girl's face, and he's just too close, invading her personal space.

Too little of it can be uncomfortable too though.

This happens for example when a guy comes up from behind a girl and makes very sudden approach without any previous interaction. She's just going to get startled.

I see this happen all the time on the dance floor and it's bad, it's not going to get you the girl or even allow you to dance with her.

So here's the rule for eye contact: if you want to approach a woman you have interest in, you want to have just enough eye contact for her to sense you coming and accept it but not so much that she's already seen you standing in a corner staring at her for the past 5 minutes building up the courage to talk to her.

In short, you will need to go talk to her within the first 3 times you make eye contact.

I know this can be tough, at first you will be like "Oh damn that's a pretty girl" then you'll think "Oh god what do I say to her" and then she'll notice you and you will panic.

So How can you train yourself to talk to a girl after making eye contact? Here's how.

It all starts as soon as you walk into a bar or a pub or even a restaurant. Start making eye contact with everyone, every member of the staff, the other guests etc. Start making all these short little interactions.

Secondly, throw in a smile too when you make eye contact. You walk past someone, you give them a little smile or a friendly nod.

And third, you can go for a high five or a wave here and there, whatever you like. Your aim here is to get to a point where you feel comfortable with all these little interactions. No matter if it's a man, a woman, a child or even a dog. You don't want to be staring at your feet the whole time.

This is also a good test to see how many people will respond positively to you, because honestly if they answer back with a smile or a high five or a wave, they are pretty much inviting you to start a conversation with them.

I'll tell you a little secret here, the way you get good at this, the way this strategy actually works, is that the more fun you are having, the better people will respond to you and the better these short interactions will go.

If you're having the time of your life people will absolutely want to high five you and talk to you. They will want to be part of the fun. If you are nervous and bored on the other hand, no one will respond even to a "Hey".

Start doing this and then you can direct it towards the women you have taken interest in.

You're in the middle of the action, you are having fun, people are noticing you, you see a girl and she's looking at you. Smile, wave if she smiles back that's it, she acknowledged you, you can walk up to her now. Maintain eye contact while you're going, maintain your smile and approach her.

You can say just about anything, your first sentence really doesn't matter as long as you don't threaten her.

"Hey we just made eye contact if I didn't say hi it would be weird right?" Just a little joke or anything along those lines "What's up I'm Steve".

Boom you're talking now.

And that's the first rule about eye contact.

CHAPTER 2:
CONVERSATION

So we are talking now, we need to escalate small talk to a proper conversation.

There's just about a million ways a conversation can take a creepy turn very quickly.

When it comes to Conversations, if you're interested in the dynamics behind a good conversation starter and how to break the ice and keep a conversation going, you should check also out my other book "BREAK THE ICE, TALK TO STRANGERS & WIN YOUR FEARS". It's available exclusively on Amazon, here on Audible and on Kindle.

What I want to focus on is the main Dos and Don'ts when talking to a girl for the first time.

The most common mistake I see men making, is with compliments. Don't get me wrong, compliments are great and they are a great way to show interest in a girl but it is all about how you compliment a woman.

Men go out and see a woman they're interested in and go "Oh my god you're so beautiful wow I've never see someone like you I'm so nervous wow!" I see this happening all the time here in L.A.

They are obviously well intentioned, they truly are nervous and they don't know what to do but what you need to understand is that every time you compliment someone, you increase the amount of tension they feel.

People will not always react positively to a compliment, things might get awkward. Have you ever been complimented for example at work? By someone who wanted a promotion maybe? Or maybe by an intern? The first thought that is going to cross your mind is "What does this person want from me?" "Why are they sweet talking me?"

What you need is a way to release the tension you create when you compliment girls. And here's how: you combine the compliment, which creates tension, with a joke to release that tension. This technique is called push-pull and it does wonders!

Be careful though, don't offend her.

Here's a good example:

"Get away from me, I can't have you around. You're way too cute and tempting"

The push-pull technique is great, practice it and excel!

CHAPTER 3:
PHYSICAL CONTACT

TOUCH.

When to touch someone you just met, where to touch someone you just met and how long to touch someone you just met are three big questions

I want to answer to in this chapter so bear with me and pay close attention.

Goldilocks rule again, not too much not too little. You need to find that perfect balance.

Repeatedly grabbing a girl, especially when you're drunk

and being really aggressive is most definitely not going to work.

Barely touching her though, can be creepy and just as bad. I know I've made this mistake in the past, I'd be talking to a girl I like and I'd sort of test her to see how she would respond to physical touch and I would just tap her on the shoulder or lightly place my hand on her shoulder.

Big mistake, this is creepy, don't do it please.

What this sort of behaviour shows is an incongruence in you: what you say and do don't match. It creates the impression that you have something to hide.

Trust me this creates a strong sense of uncomfortableness in the girl.

How do you touch the right way?

Well, first off, there is not just one correct way to do it.

Once you get a certain level of social awareness you could probably just walk over to a girl, give her a hug, grab her, spin her around and dance with her no problem.

But this is something I would not suggest because without that strong sense of social awareness you might run into some problems and offend/scare people.

The safest way, which is what I strongly recommend, would be to try this early enough in the interaction: once you are talking to a girl, touch her somewhere on her arm, between 1 and 3 seconds.

Here in the US, this is generally a safe gesture. You'll be fine, it's really not that long.

It's the perfect amount of time to see how receptive she

is to you.

Here's a random scenario, you've been talking to her for a bit and decide to grab a drink, touch her arm, rest your hand there for a few seconds and say "Hey me and my friends are gonna go over to the bar to grab a drink, do you want to come with us?" and take your hand off her arm.

It's simple, there's no reason to over think this sort of interactions.

With enough practice it will come naturally for you.

If she says something along the lines of "Sure let's go" then grabs your hand and walks to the bar with you… well I've great news for you she's not just comfortable touching you, she's definitely interested.

If she replies that she wants to stay there it can mean a

couple different things: maybe she's not feeling comfortable enough with you just yet, or it may just be the way she is or maybe she's in a bad mood or she doesn't like the color of your shoes or simply that she doesn't want you touching her.

From this point you can do two things:

Either you end it there and move on onto another girl you like or go back to talking to her with less touching and see if you two connect at all.

You can try again after a few minutes with the 1 to 3 seconds touch technique.

If things don't change, hey she might just not be a match. It's time to move on.

This is how you should act when it comes to physical contact, 1 to 3 seconds are generally safe but remember you have to pick up the feedback you receive from the girl and react accordingly.

This is to avoid creepiness and awkwardness.

CHAPTER 4:
ESCAPING

In this fourth chapter I want to talk to you about something us men tend not to realize.

The feeling of being trapped by someone or having no escape route open to us.

If you're a guy you would usually not experience this in a pick up scenario: most women are going to be smaller than you, even if they are the same height as you or taller, you will most likely be physically stronger and they would lose to you in a fight, am I right?

They'll weight less or be shorter etc.

All of this makes you quite literally a physical threat to them! This is why over thousands of years women have evolved this sense of danger and creepiness from men they don't know. It's a visceral feeling of unsafeness.

This is why you can now easily imagine that if you happen to trap them physically in a small place, even if you don't realize it and even if you're just talking to them and the conversation is going well, they will feel threatened. They will think "Oh gosh I have to get out of here", unless she has a VERY sense of comfort with you which is something you will not achieve in the first few minutes together.

The other day I saw a guy and a girl, they were talking, it looked like their conversation was flowing. At some point he goes "Hey let's sit down over here", they sit at a booth, she slides in first and he goes second. Terrible decision, everything is ruined. He has just trapped her in this booth and she doesn't consciously realize it but she immediately goes "Oh I need to get out of here" "I need to go to the bathroom" "I need to find my friends". She wants to run away.

It would be the same at the bar or in a club, a guy walks up to a girl, he places himself between the bar and the exit. He's not physically blocking her only escape route.

This is a big mistake that's going to most likely cost you that girl.

Don't trap girls, pay attention to where you are standing or sitting. Put your own back against the wall, go first inside the tiny booth alright? This will give her a sense of security because she knows she can just walk away as soon as she needs to. You will need to arrange things this way: don't trap, it's simple.

Always make sure you are the one who is going to have a hard time exiting rather than her.

These are the 4 pillars you will need to follow to flirt with girls and avoid being creepy.

I once again praise you for taking action and studying this mini guide, let me know how it goes.

I wish you all the best.

CONCLUSION

Improving our ability to read and understand others is an incredibly serious step we all need to make in order to improve ourselves and to reach our objectives.

Flirting is a skill and as such it must be acquired and practiced.

Remember, when you are trying to build a skill, you're trying to rewire your brain, create new neural pathways.

This takes a lot of willpower.

Be patient and keep trying. The results will come in no time bringing nothing but positive responses from the people around you.

Improving your technique using the methods I illustrated in this book will do wonders.

Get back in action and let me know how it goes.

Try out these tricks and improve!

Best of luck see you in the next book.

ACKNOWLEDGEMENTS

The purpose of our books is to make your life better by improving the very fundamental way you learn new things and clear your confusion and bad habits.

We want to thank you for taking action by reading this book and we hope that you keep on using these simple and efficient methods in order to reach your goal. If you found this helpful, we hope that you can spread the word to everyone around you who struggles with the same problems in order to help them.

We also want to thank all of the members of our publishing team for making this possible.

A special thanks goes also to all of the researchers who study this matter every day at the cost of their own sleep to help us improve our life.

Thank you all.